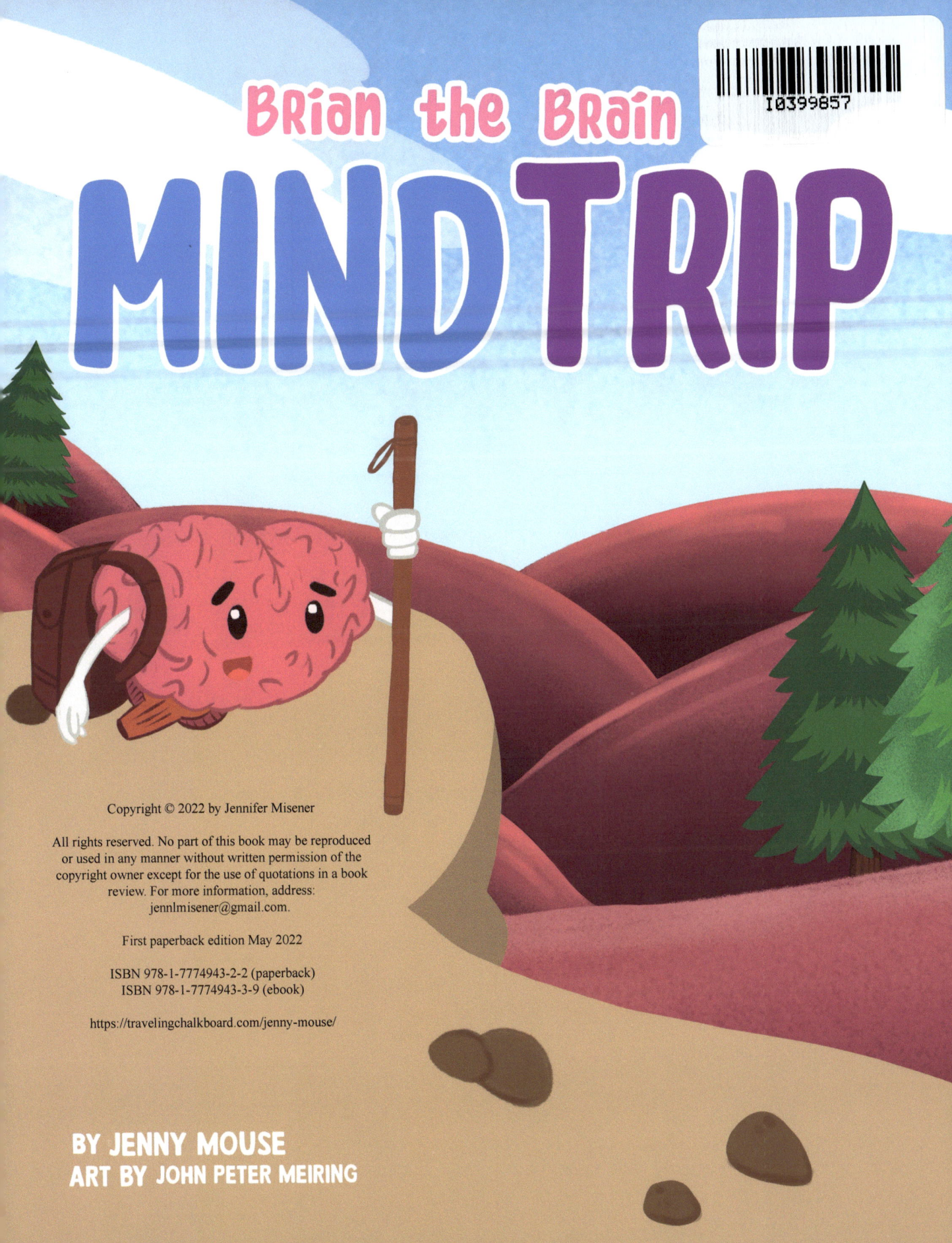

Brian the Brain
MINDTRIP

Copyright © 2022 by Jennifer Misener

All rights reserved. No part of this book may be reproduced or used in any manner without written permission of the copyright owner except for the use of quotations in a book review. For more information, address: jennlmisener@gmail.com.

First paperback edition May 2022

ISBN 978-1-7774943-2-2 (paperback)
ISBN 978-1-7774943-3-9 (ebook)

https://travelingchalkboard.com/jenny-mouse/

BY JENNY MOUSE
ART BY JOHN PETER MEIRING

About the Author

Jenny Mouse is the mom of two science-loving kids! She lives in Ontario, Canada, and loves passing the long winters creating stories and doing experiments. She is passionate about mental health and wants to make sure everyone realizes how important their brain is!

Dedications:
For Felix and Lucy.

With special thanks to my husband Nathan, and my good friend Sarah.

About the Illustrator

John Peter is an illustrator and animator who lives in London, England, surrounded by the River Thames and lovely forests. After studying Advertising Design, he started doing drawings for companies and animating for the creative industries until he found out that illustrating for children is such a wonderful field. He prefers creating illustrations digitally on his graphic tablets, always trying to hide the pen from his crafty but adorable dog.

https://www.oddpumpkinstudio.com

About the Subject Matter Expert

Robin Katz has a post-professional Doctorate in Occupational Therapy (OT) from Boston University (2012) as well as a Masters of Social Work from Wurzweiler School of Social Work (2006). Since becoming a licensed OT in 1981, she has taught about the brain as part of her clinical work with children and during her years as an occupational therapy faculty member.

Hey, there! I'm Brian. I'm a brain, and I'm going on a trip.

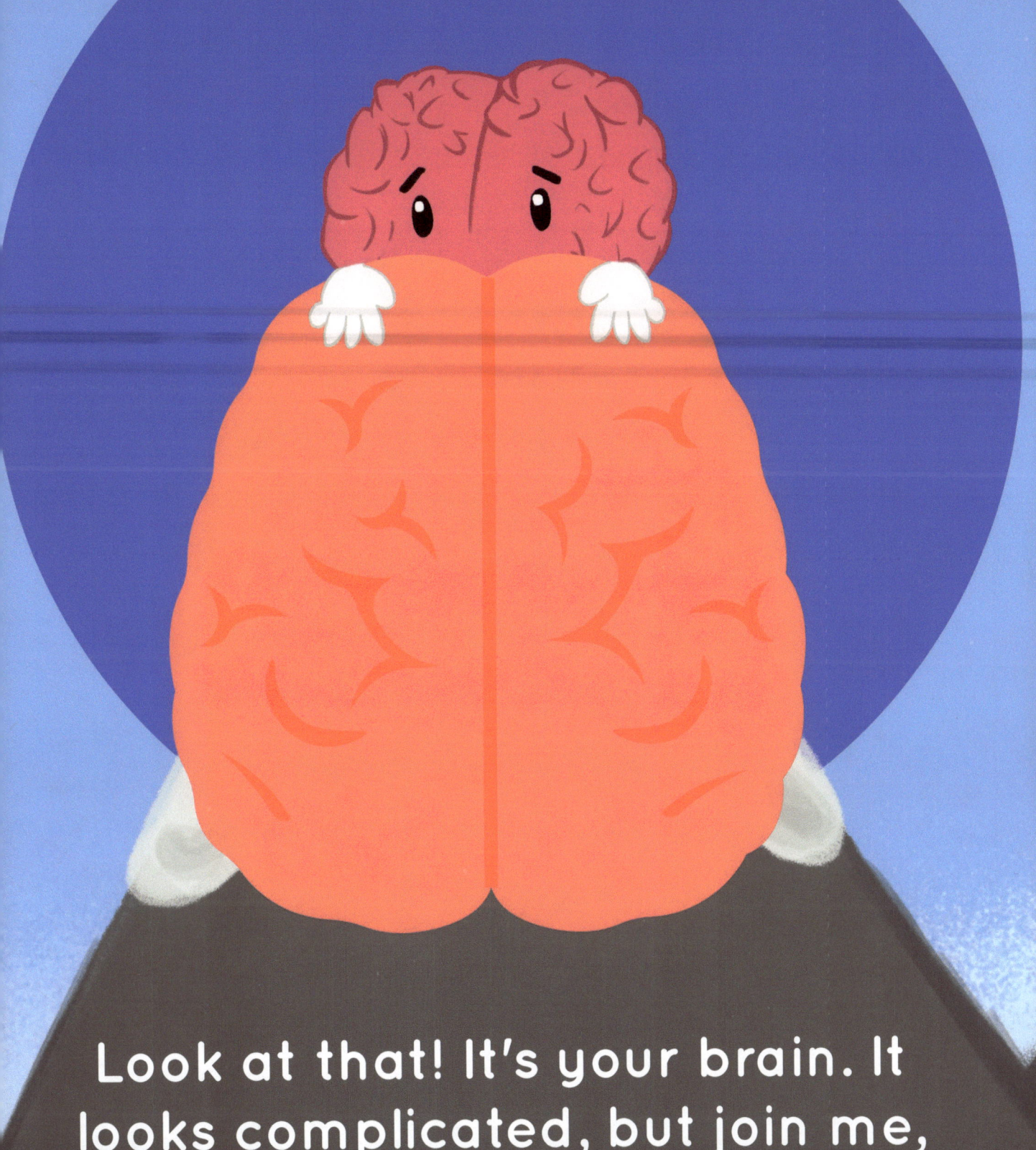

Look at that! It's your brain. It looks complicated, but join me, and I'll teach you all about it.

The brain has three main parts that we will explore.

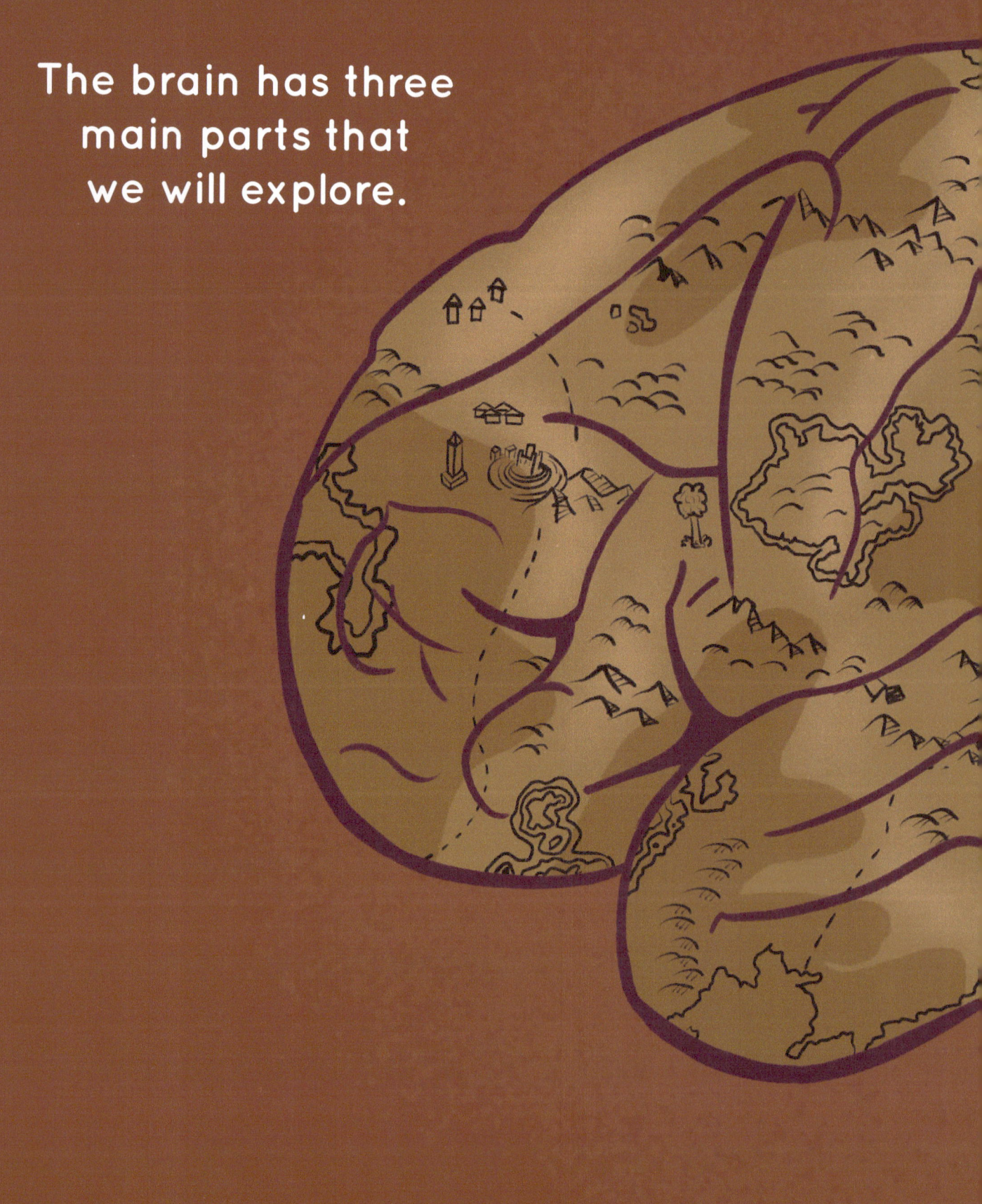

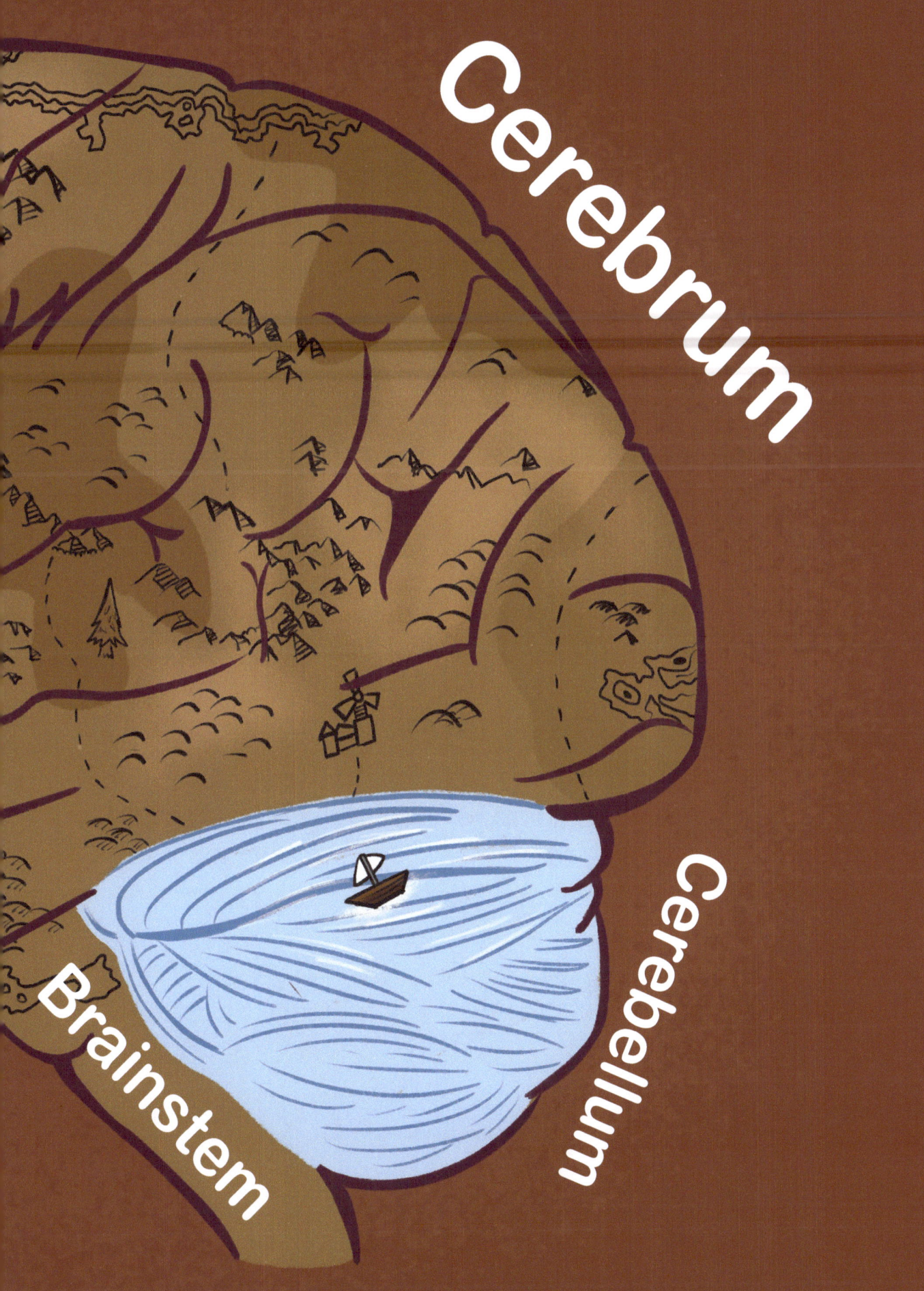

Brainstem

You are here!

The brainstem is always busy. Even when you're sleeping, it is still working.

While you sleep, it keeps your heart, lungs, and stomach working.

Watch out for stormy seas!

It's a good thing your cerebellum helps control posture and balance!

The bumps give your brain more room for memories and provide enough space for the brain to do everything it needs to do!

GYRUS

GYRUS

SULCUS

Each valley is called a sulcus.
(SUL-kus)

The cerebrum has two sides! They are called the right and left hemispheres.

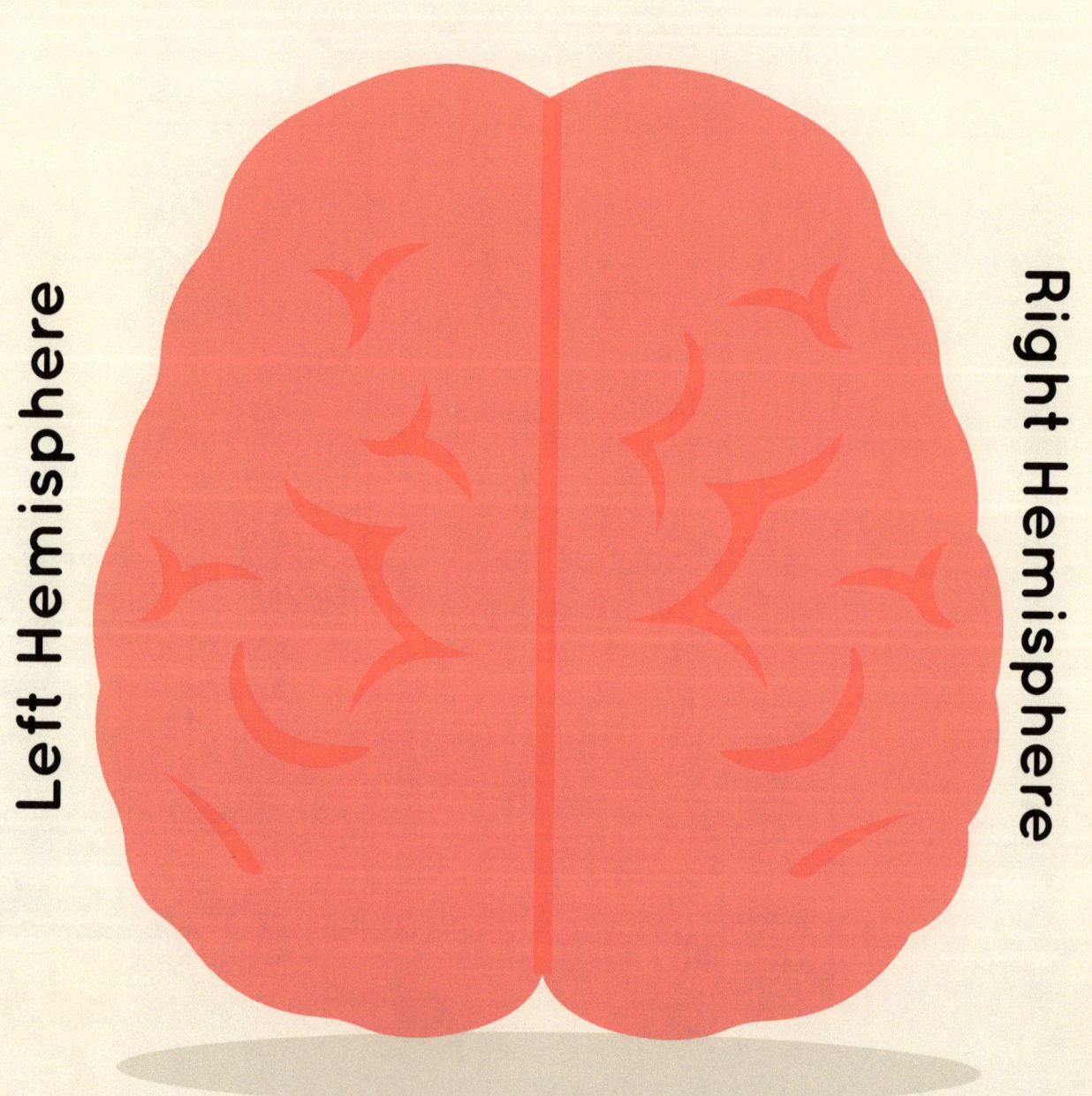

Both of them contain a frontal lobe, a parietal lobe, a temporal lobe, and an occipital lobe.

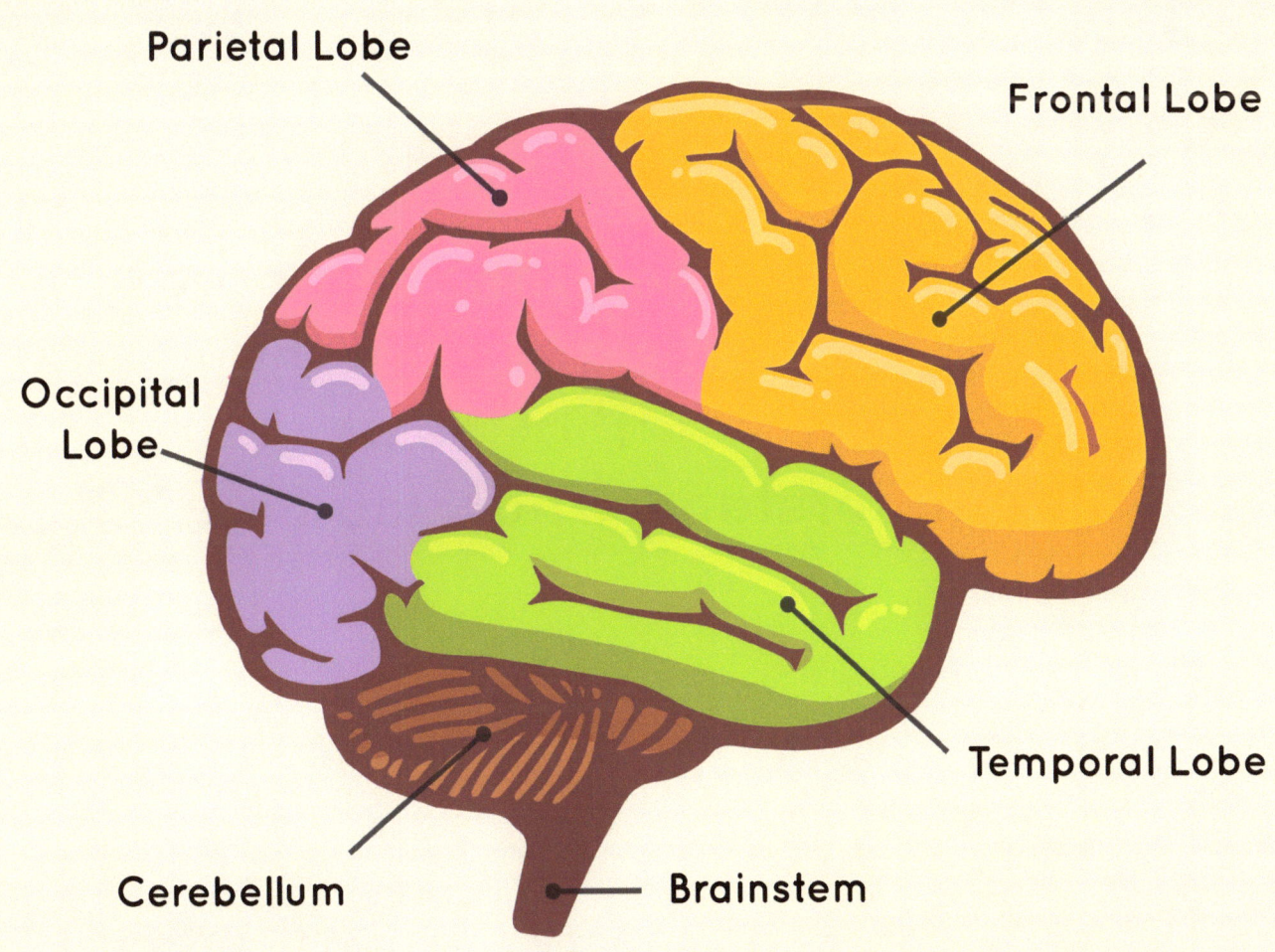

WOW! Look at this place! We're under the cerebral cortex now. It's the lumpy structure with all the hills.

And we've found the limbic system. Remember the brainstem we saw earlier? We're right on top of it!

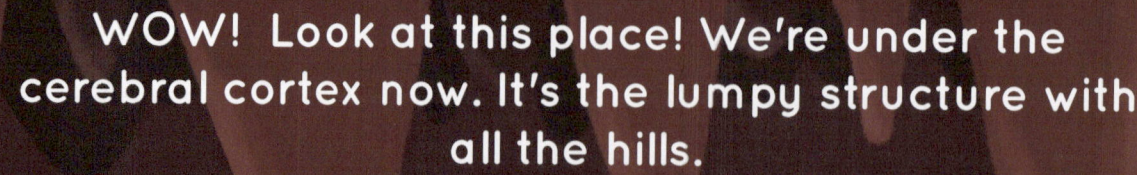

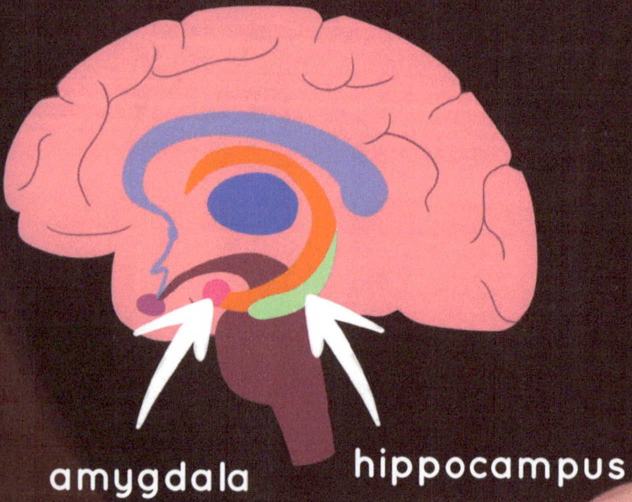

amygdala   hippocampus

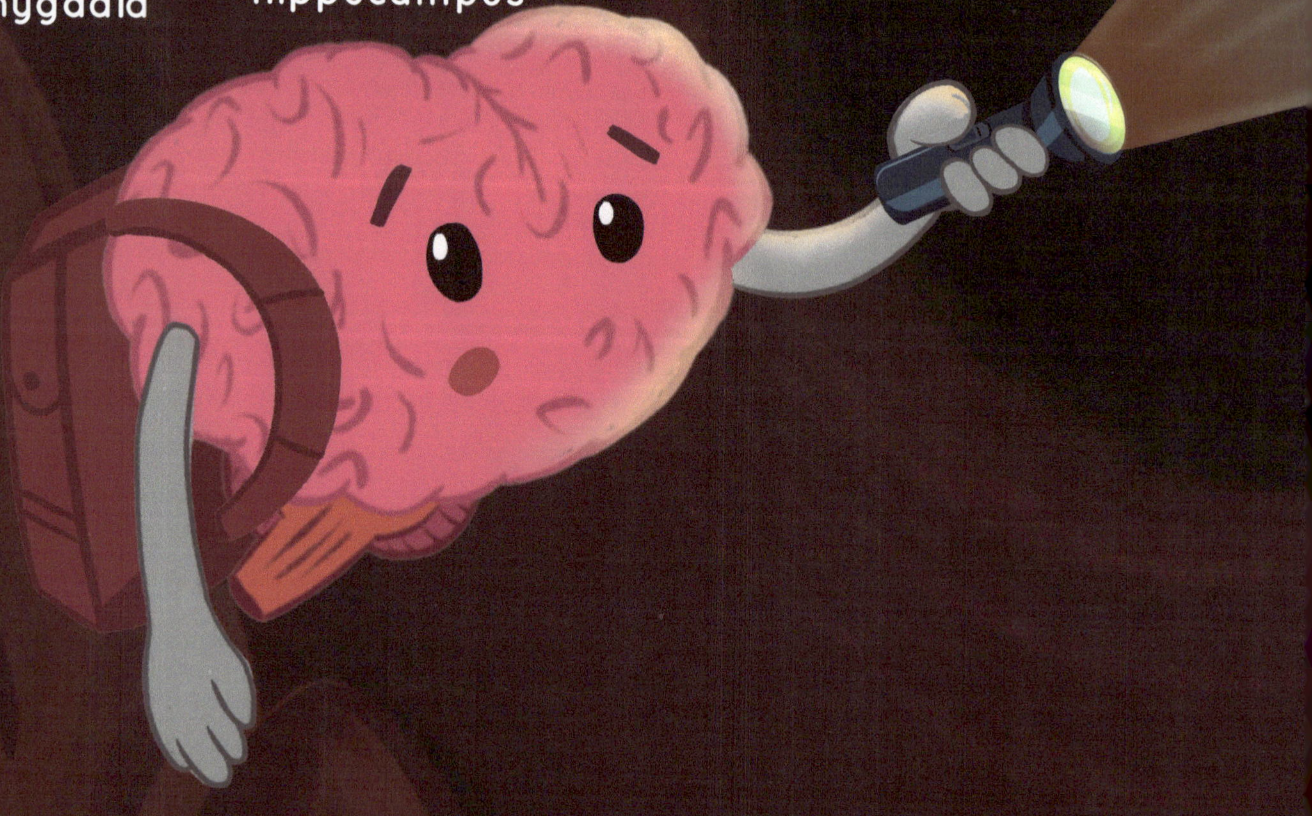

Now, we're deep inside the temporal lobe. The hippocampus is 'Memory Lane' because this part of the limbic system helps you store your memories.

Hey, we just landed in the prefrontal cortex. It's the part of the frontal cortex that helps us manage our impulses. So, let's find someone in control.

YOU ARE HERE.

Frontal Lobe

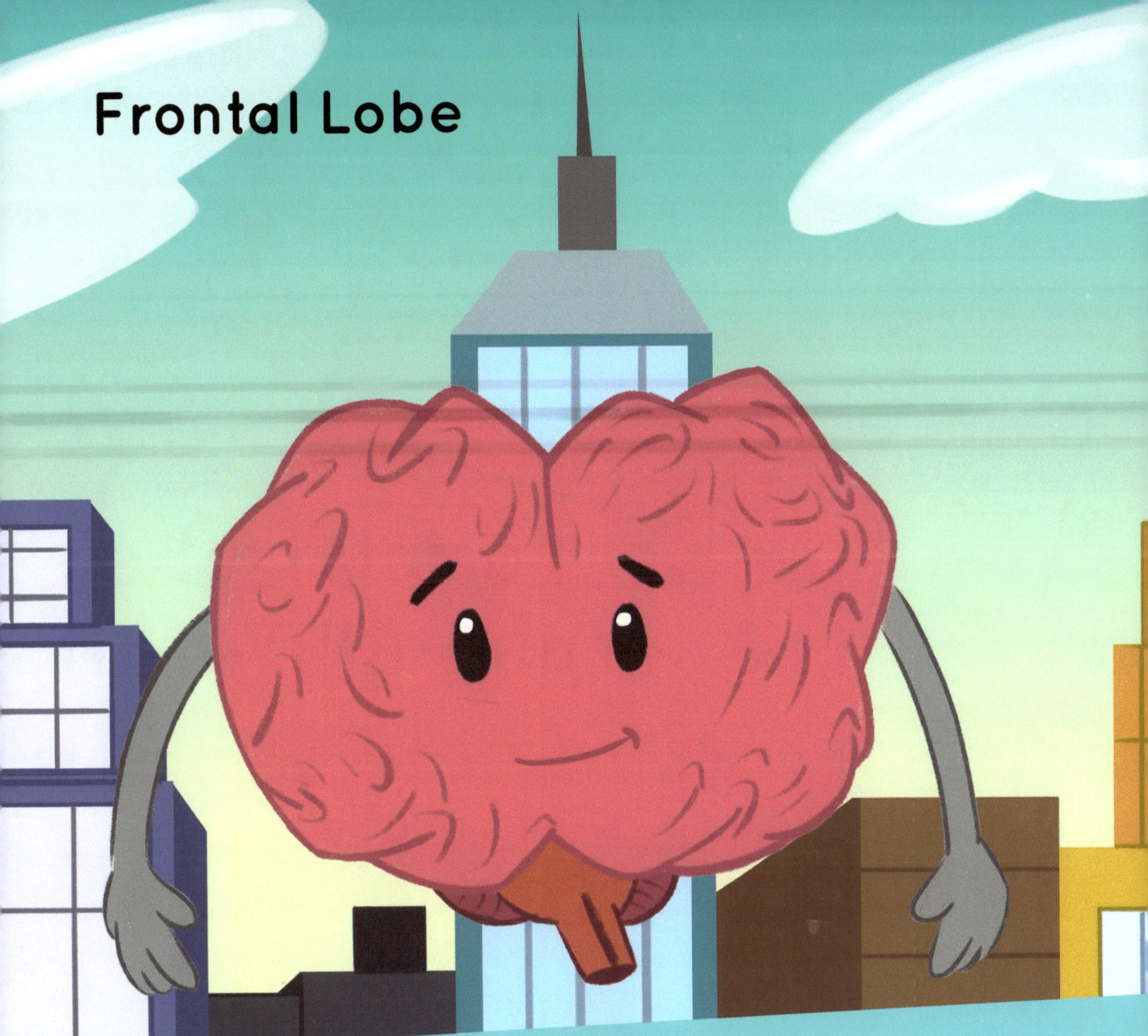

A frontal lobe is a control center!
It helps with planning body movements and controlling our behavior to get stuff done. But when it's not working at its best, we can lose emotional control, and then we need to calm down.

It was fun visiting the 'city,' but let's get back to the 'country!'

Parietal lobe (puh-RIHY-e-tl)

A parietal lobe is all about sensations. This place has it all!

Feeling objects that are soft, cold, or hard can help us calm down.

We made it to this occipital lobe! It's the most beautiful place because it helps us understand what we see with our eyes. Okay, it's time to call it a day!

Join us next time to strengthen your connections.

www.ingramcontent.com/pod-product-compliance
Lightning Source LLC
Chambersburg PA
CBHW040022130526
44590CB00036B/64